REMEMBERING . . .
The Good Old Days

REMEMBERING . . .
The Good Old Days

By

Marge Knoth

© Copyright 1989, 1995 by Marge Knoth

ALL RIGHTS RESERVED

No part of this book may be reproduced
in any form or by any electronic means
without written permission from the author.

ISBN   0-927935-09-2

First printing: July, 1989
Second printing: February, 1990
Third printing: November, 1990
Fourth printing: March, 1991
Fifth printing: September, 1993
Sixth printing: October, 1995

DEDICATION

Remembering the Good Old Days is dedicated to all those very special people, many in our nursing homes today, who lived through the era written about in this book. It is especially dedicated to the residents of Comfort Retirement and Nursing Home in Lafayette, Indiana who contributed much of the information presented here while they reminisced every Tuesday morning over coffee and donuts about the days between 1890 and 1945.

NOTE FROM THE AUTHOR

Though years of research have gone into this book, much of the information has come directly from the interviewing of older residents, most of whom live in nursing homes. Therefore, it cannot be considered *entirely* factual, and the author does not claim it to be so, though much effort has gone into making it as factual as possible. The purpose of this book is simply to enable you to get your residents actively remembering and eagerly sharing about their past life--the way they remember it. And as you do, you will often find residents remembering the same happenings in entirely different ways with many discrepancies in their stories. That is to be expected and serves to make your group more lively. As you use this book, I wish you many happy hours of reminiscing. May the Good Lord richly bless each and every one of you and your residents.

TABLE OF CONTENTS

Section 1

Section 2

Section 5

SPECIAL HELPS FOR
ACTIVITY DIRECTORS

SECTION 1

1

THE OLD HOME PLACE

Remember the home of your childhood?
What did it look like?
Was it in the country or the city?
Was it big or small?
Was it made of wood, brick or stone?
Did it have lots of trees around it?
Did you have a swing in one tree?
What other buildings were around the house?
Where did you sleep?
Where did you play?
Did you have a dog?
What was his name?
Did you have other animals?
What was the kitchen like?
Did it have an old pump on the sink?
What kind of table did you have?
Did it have a checkered oilcloth on it?
What usually set in the middle of the table?
Was it a spoon holder?
What did it look like?
What kind of stove did you have in the kitchen?

Did you have any chores associated that stove?

Would you like to see that old house today?

2

THE 500 RACE

Do you remember the first 500 mile race at Indianapolis?

When was it held? (1911)

What did those first race cars look like?

Did they not have real bodies, but rather just a hood covering and a
  gasoline tank mounted behind the driver?

How many seats did those first race cars have?

Wasn't it usually two?

Who was the second seat for?

Was it the mechanic who rode along?

Do you know who won that first race?

Was it Ray Harroun?

Do you know how fast the average speed was? (74 mph)

What was a nickname for the 500 track? (brickyard)

Before the track was lined with brick, how was it paved? (limestone)

What problems do you think that caused?

Do you think there was a lot of dust?

Do you remember cigar-smoking Barney O'Field?

Remember how he was a daredevil?

Remember what he raced against? -- cars, horses, even airplanes.

When was the 100 mile per hour record broken? (1925)

Did the track close during World Wars I and World War II? (yes)

Do you know where the very first recorded race was held?

Wasn't it between Chicago and Evanston?

How fast do you think the drivers went? (5 mph)

Would you have liked to drive a race car?

3

THE CHAUTAUQUA

What was the chautauqua?
Was it a traveling show?
Did you ever see one?
What acts were featured?
Were there Indian shows, magicians, yodelers, opera singers, bands,
    plays, concerts and preachers?
Did you ever hear Billy Sunday?
Where did the chautauqua get its name?
Was it from Lake Chautauqua in New York where it originated?
When did the traveling show finally end?
Was it when the Model T became popular?

4

NICKELODEON

What was the nickelodeon?
Was it first a motion picture theater?
How much did it cost to see?
Was it five cents for 500 to 800 feet of film lasting about 15 minutes?
Before the nickelodeon, what form of entertainment was relied upon?
Was it vaudeville?
What is vaudeville?
Who do you think were the biggest fans of the nickelodeon? (middle-
    aged women)
Do you remember any signs in those lobbies?
What did they say?

Did they read something like, "Don't spit on the floor" and "Don't use bad language"?

Some people thought of the nickelodeon as a jukebox? Did you?

5

SPORTS LONG AGO

Did you play sports long ago?

Were they different than today's?

How was basketball different?

What did you use for nets?

Was it wooden peach baskets?

Were there any backboards?

Remember how the game was played in three periods of 20 minutes each?

Remember how there were foul-shooting specialists?

Remember how low scoring those games were--like eight to ten?

How did you get to your ball games?

Did you ever ride the interurban?

Did you ever play baseball?

What was "town and country"?

Was "town" infield and "country" outfield?

Remember when bases were not run?

Remember when you just batted the ball and tried to run to a point and back before the other players hit you with the ball and got you out?

Did you play any other games?

What were they?

6

SHAME, SHAME

Did girls ever become pregnant long ago without being married?
Was it thought really bad?
How did they handle the situation?
Did they stay at home or did they sometimes go to an aunt's to live?
What were some ways a gal kept others from knowing?
Did she bind her belly tight?
Were these girls ever scorned or ridiculed?
What would happen to the father of the baby?
Was he ridiculed or not?

7

WOMEN'S RIGHTS

Do you remember women trying to win the right to vote?
Do you remember any big parades in New York for that purpose?
What was the universal sign that women were for the cause of women
    voting?
Was it the yellow daisy, jonquil or buttercup worn as a corsage?
Were fathers often against mothers and daughters voting?
Did her vote for the opposition cancel out his vote?
When did women gain the right to vote? (1919)
Do you remember names like *Lucretia Coffin Mott, Elizabeth Cady
    Stanton* and *Susan B. Anthony?*
Were they big in the women's rights movement?
Do you remember the very first time you voted?
Where was it?
How did you get there?
How did you vote?

Did it feel like a real freedom?
Did your mother vote when she received the privilege?

8

ZIEGFIELD FOLLIES

Do you know who Florenz Ziegfield was?
What were the Ziegfield Follies?
Were they long lines of dancing girls who performed for audiences?
When a gal became one of the girls, was her reputation subject to question?
What did these girls wear?
Was it feathers and chiffon?
What else was required of them to be a Ziegfield girl?
Wasn't it to have a good figure, pretty hair and good teeth?
Did you ever see the follies?
Was Will Rogers ever affiliated with them?

9

THE GIBSON GIRL

Have you ever heard of the *Gibson Girl?*
Did your mother ever talk of her?
Who was she?
Was she even real?
Wasn't she just a series of pen and ink drawings that showed an ideal women doing many things?
What was she portrayed doing in the drawings?
Wasn't it things like nursing sick soldiers, being a nun, being made more beautiful by a maid, or painting at an easel in an open field?

What were her clothes like?

Weren't they modest, high-necked, long flowing gowns, yet very fashionable.

Did women want to model themselves after the Gibson Girl? Why?

Where was her picture found?

Wasn't it on hair brushes, mirrors, china plates, broom handles, pillows and silverware?

When was she popular?

Was it.around 1890 to 1900?

10

SEWING IN THE OLD DAYS

Remember sewing long ago?

Did you sew by hand, or did you have a machine?

What kind?

How was it powered?

Was it electric or foot-powered?

What did you sew on it?

Did you make everything, even dish towels and underwear?

Where did you get the material?

Did you ever use feed sacks?

Did you use overall cloth?

What about gingham, percale and muslin?

What did you sew from muslin?

Did you make your own sheets?

When a sheet wore out in the middle, how did you mend it?

Did you ever get together with other women to sew?

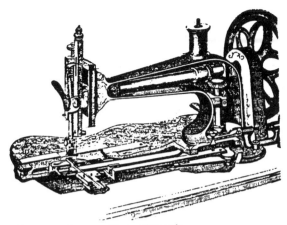

Singer sewing machine. *Harper's*

11

STREET CARS AND INTERURBANS

Ever ride a street car?
Where did it take you?
How much did it cost?
What did it look like?
What did it smell like?
Was it ozone gas?
What type of seats did it have?
Were they wicker?
Were there summer and winter cars?
Did street cars ever slide down hills on icy days?
Where was your street car garage located?
Do you remember the interurban?
How were they different?
How did you let the conductor know you wanted off?
Did you ever ride the street car to ball games?
When did street cars go out of service in your city?
Why were they no longer needed?

12

GETTING HITCHED LONG AGO

Remember those weddings of long ago?

Do you remember yours?

What was it like?

Where was it held?

Was it large or small?

What did you wear?

Did you go for a ride after the ceremony?

What means of transportation did you use?

Do you remember some brides being pushed around the downtown
square in a wheelbarrow, or being pulled by painted horses?

Where did you go for a honeymoon?

What is a chivaree?

Did you have one?

When you were at home sleeping, did guests stand outside your house
and ring bells and bang pan lids?

Did you invite them in for refreshments?

Did anyone play wedding tricks on you--tricks like bothering your
suitcase, putting live chickens in your house, making your bed fall
down when you got in, or filling your bed with beans or salt?

Were weddings a time of special fun long ago?

Did people take these pranks in good humor?

What else do you remember about your wedding?

13

WPA

Do you remember the WPA?

What was it?

What did its name mean?

Was it the *Works Progress Administration* at first?

Was that name changed?

Do you remember what it was next called in 1939?

Was it the *Works Projects Administration?*

Why was it changed?

Was it because projects were given to put people to work rather than just provide handouts?

Did you ever work for the WPA?

Did you know anyone who did?

How much money did you or they make?

What job did you, or they do?

What other kind of jobs were available?

Was it building sidewalks, outdoor toilets and roads?

Were some people paid to dance, perform or paint?

When did it start? (1935)

What president started the WPA? (FDR)

How many were employed at one time? (8.5 million)

Do you think the WPA was a good thing?

Do you think we should have something like it today?

14

FARMING LONG AGO

Did you ever farm with horses?

What were their names?

How was that different than farming with tractors?

Were fields smaller in those days than today?

What is a hand-held corn planter?

Remember the big steam engines?

What was the first internal combustion engine tractor?

Was it the *Case?*

What are some of the other early tractors?

Do you remember the *Hornsley-Akroyed,* the *Twin City-Avery,* the *International Harvester* and the *Waterloo Boy?*

How about the *Rumley Model E* that went into production in 1911 weighing 26,000 pounds?

What tractor did Henry Ford make?

Was it the *Fordson?*

Do you know how much it weighed?

Wasn't it just 1500 pounds?

Did Ford become very successful in the tractor market?

How many tractors did he produce? Wasn't it 100,000 or 50% of the world's production?

Remember the *Silver Grip* tractor between 1917 and 1923 by General Motors, and the *Sampson Model M,* a four cylinder, water cooled petrol/paraffin engine?

Could you plow more land in a day with tractors than with horses?

Remember how the tractor could plow as much land in an hour as a team of five horse could plow all day?

Remember how with tractors farmers could get their seeds in the ground up to two weeks earlier?

Do you remember when tractors first got lights?

What kind were they?

Were they acetylene gas lights--one on the front and one on the rear?

Was it easier farming with tractors than with horses?

Page 22

15

EARLY TELEVISION

Remember the first time you saw a T.V.?

What did it look like?

Were you surprised?

How was the screen shaped?

Was it round or rectangular?

When did you get your first TV set?

When did TV first come in? (1931)

How far was the broadcasting radius then? (15 miles)

Do you remember any early programs?

How about *Amos and Andy*, *Kukla and Ollie* and the *Marks Brothers*?

Remember *Gene Autry, Roy Rogers* and *Hit Parade*?

How about *Howdy Doody, Young Dr. Malone* and the *Ed Sullivan* show?

Remember TV lights?

What were they?

Where did they set?

How did you make your black and white TV appear colored?

Did you put a hard plastic sheet against the screen that was green at the bottom, blue at the top and yellow in the middle?

16

THE SPEAKEASIES

What is a speakeasy?

Was it a bar that sold booze illegally during prohibition?

Did you ever know of one?

Did you ever go to one?

Did they have bad reputations?
Did you need a password to get in? Why?
Were they ever raided?
How did they hide all the booze before the police got there?
Did prostitution go on at some of these establishments?
How did you dress when you went to a speakeasy?
Did criminals hang out there?

17
THE ROARING TWENTIES

(see "We Remember the Twenties", page 124)

Remember the roaring '20's?
What made them special?
Was it a wild time? innocent time?
Remember pogo sticks, sea baths and crossword puzzle books?
Remember victrolas, player pianos and war books?
Were these war books kept hidden? Why?
What presidents reigned during the '20's?
Weren't there four--Wilson, Harding, Hoover and Coolidge?
Remember the *Zeppelin?*
What was it?
What fashions did women wear?
What was a flapper dress?
Did you ever wear one?
What accessories were worn with it?
Why were watches worn on the thigh?
Were bosoms made flat and how? Why?
Remember camiknickers that were drawers plus chemise usually in
    pink silk?
How were eyebrows worn?
Were they plucked thin?

What was the cloche hat?

What kind of hair styles were popular?

What were the popular cuts?

Remember the *Egyptian* and the *shingle* bob?

How did you get your hair permed?

What were those monster machines like that frizzed the hair?

What was the favorite dance of the 20's?

Were moral standards lower then than before that time?

Were they a fun time?

18

THE PLAYER PIANO

What is a player piano?

Did you ever have one?

How did it work?

Was it a vacuum or an air-pump operated by a foot pedal?

Did you have to know how to play it?

Was there a special roll of paper for it?

What did this paper look like?

Did it have holes punched in it?

Did the piano have a glass front?

Have you ever heard of turning an antique pipe organ into a pump organ by attaching a vacuum cleaner to it?

Remember the leisurely Sunday afternoons around that old piano?

Remember how you all sang together and had fun?

In what room was this old piano kept?

Would you like to have one today?

19

THE THRILLING THIRTIES

Remember the 1930's?

Were they a happy or sad time?

Weren't they both?

What do you best remember about the '30's?

Was it the Great Depression?

How did you survive tough times?

Remember the dance-a-thons?

How did women wear their hair?

Wasn't it long and glamorous after the short bobs of the '20's?

Remember how women's hats were being shed?

Remember how some still wore hats but at ridiculous angles?

Remember the 10-cent chain letter?

What kind of hose did women wear?

Did they have seams?

What fashions did women wear?

Were they long sleek evening gowns, beach pajamas, and backless swim suits?

What did men wear?

Remember the light grey tweed jackets and blazers?

How about polka-dot bow ties and suede shoes?

What dancers entertained folks?

Remember Ginger Rogers and Fred Astaire?

What was the most famous movie of all time then?

Remember *Gone With the Wind*?

Remember how the hottest summer and the coldest winter were in 1937?

Was there a great flood in 1937?

What was it like?

What are your major memories of the '30's?

20

WILL ROGERS

Do you remember Will Rogers?

Who was he?

How did he become famous?

What jobs did he have?

Wasn't he a restless roper, actor, speaker, columnist and cowboy philosopher?

Was he well-liked? Why?

What did he look like?

What did he sound like?

Did he have a good heart?

Didn't he discreetly give large amounts of money to needy causes?

Did he sing?

Who was his wife?

Was it Betty Blake?

Did he ever lose sight of his simple roots?

Did he relate to the common people or the famous?

Wasn't it both?

Didn't he humorously put down presidents, other politicians and
famous people--and get away with it?

Can you remember any famous saying of his?

Did he love his fellow man from the heart?

Did he ever do commercials?

How about for *Bull Durham* tobacco?

Did you ever see Will Rogers?

SECTION 2

21

DANCE MARATHONS

Did you ever attend a dance marathon?

What was it?

How much did it cost?

What was the purpose of it?

Did couples enter and plan to dance for a long time?

What happened to couples feet?

Did they swell really bad?

How long did they dance?

How long did the marathons last?

Wasn't it sometimes for days on end?

Didn't they go till they fell down?

Remember how one partner would hold up the other sleeping one and drag him or her around the dance floor like a rag doll?

What kind of songs did they dance to?

Were they songs like *Let Me Call You Sweetheart?*

What was the prize?

Wasn't it quite a bit of money? (sometimes $5000)

When were the dances popular?

Wasn't it during the 20's and 30's?

22

TOM MIX

Who was Tom Mix?

Wasn't he a favorite cowboy movie star that kids looked up to?

What was his favorite saying?

Was it "Reach to the sky? Law breakers always lose. Shoot straight.
Straight shooters always win. It pays to shoot straight"?

Did he have a fan club?

Remember how you, as children, had to pledge to shoot straight with
parents by obeying and by eating the food put before you?

Remember how kids promised to shoot straight with Tom Mix by
eating at least three bowls of Ralston cereal a week?

Did Tom Mix receive many injuries on screen?

Wasn't it 47 injuries--stabbed 22 times, shot 12, and blown up once--
to name a few?

How many films did Tom Mix make?

Can you guess? (180)

Was his real life as straight as he portrayed on the screen? (no)

23

RAISING CHICKENS

Did you ever raise chickens?

How many?

Did you live in the country or in town?

Did you hatch them from eggs?

Did the old hen sit on the eggs?

Was there any trick to make her sit when she didn't want to?

Did you ever put a glass egg in her nest to make her sit?

Did the rooster ever take over her job of sitting on the nest?

Did you ever feed your chickens broken up porcelain plates? Why?
Did you ever get several hundred baby chicks from the brooder?
How did you keep them warm?
What was a caponized bird?
Was it one who had his testicles removed?
Did you ever dress a chicken?
How did you kill it?
Did it ever run around after its head was cut off?
Why would the bird be dipped in hot water?
What was the most chickens you ever dressed in one day?

24

HOME REMEDIES

Were you ever sick as a child?
Did you always call the doctor?
Did your mother have some home remedies?
What were some of them?
How was a cold treated?
Was it with goose grease rubbed on the chest, the palms of the hands, and the soles of the feet?
Did you ever have a red rag or an old sock tied around your neck?
How were cobwebs used for healing?
Weren't they applied to stop bleeding?
How were hiccups cured?
One way was to eat a spoon of sugar or peanut butter.
How was ringworm treated?
Was it by squeezing juice from fallen black walnut hulls and rubbing it on the spot?
What did you do for rheumatism?
Did you ever let a bee sting the affected area?
Did you ever kill a rattlesnake, skin it, put its skin in a jug of corn whiskey and drink it?

Was smoke ever blown in your ear? Why?
Was it to treat an earache?
How was a boil treated?
Was a piece of fat taped over it to cause it to come to a head?
Were ingrown toenails cured the same way?
How would a sore eye be treated?
Did you ever put a slice of bread that had been soaked in milk on it,
    and was it held in place with an old stocking?
Did you ever have a mustard plaster?
What was that?
What other remedies did you use?

25

LITTLE PESTS

Did you ever have little pests long ago?
What about flies?
How did you kill them?
Did you ever use flypaper?
What was that?
How did it work?
How did it smell?
Did you ever make a fly trap with a glass of soapy water and put a
    cardboard top on it with some jam on it?
Do you know of a plant called the "Venus fly trap"?
How did you treat mosquitoes?
What, before screens, was put on the windows for protection from
    them?
Was it called mosquito netting?
What did it look like?
When babies were outside in their cribs for fresh air, was the crib
    covered with this netting?
What was oil of citronella?

Was it rubbed on the skin to protect against mosquitos?
How did you fight cockroaches?
Did you ever use *Borax* or cucumber rinds?
What were cockroach houses?
Did you ever have bugs in your flour?
Were there ever rats in your house?
How was lice treated?
Did you rub a mixture of lard and sulphur or kerosene into the head?

26

NEIGHBORS

Did you have good neighbors long ago?
What were their names?
Did they have children your age?
Why were they good neighbors?
Did they ever help you? How?
Did you help them?
How did a neighbor help when someone died?
How did they help one another in farming?
Did they ever work together to build barns for one another?
Did you ever have help building a barn?
Did you return the favor?
Did you butcher together?
How did you divide the work and the meat?
Did women neighbors ever get together? Why?
Was it for sewing purposes?

27

CHILDBIRTH LONG AGO

Did you ever have babies?
Where did you give birth to them?
Did you have girls or boys?
Did you have a doctor present for their births?
Who else helped you?
Did you go to a hospital?
Did you ever pay your doctor with anything other than money?
What was it called when one was expecting?
Was it sometimes called "being in a family way" or "confinement" or
    "being in a delicate condition"?
What did you do for maternity clothes?
Did you ever just set pieces in your clothes to expand them?
What were "mother hubbard" dresses?
Did you ever use a midwife?
Did you know any?
Was it fashionable in the '30's to have babies in hospitals?
How much did it cost?
Was it 25 to 35% of an average working man's income?
Were hospitals considered safe?
What was twilight sleep?
Did you ever help deliver a baby?

28

BRIDGES

Can you remember any particular bridges in your town that were there
    when you were young?
What did they look like?

Were they covered bridges?
Tell me about covered bridges?
Why did they have a top on them?
How were they lit?
Were they dark inside?
Were they a fire hazard?
Did you ever park a buggy under the bridge to spoon?
Do you remember any bridges coming down in floods?
Do you like to see covered bridges today?
Did you ever ride a ferry boat across when the bridge was out?

29

GOING INTO THE WOODS

Do you ever remember going into the woods?
Why did you go there?
Did you ever gather food there?
What kind?
Did you find berries?
What kind?
What did you find for Christmas in the woods?
Did you chop down your own tree?
Did you ever gather red berries there?
Did you ever go mushroom hunting?
What about hunting?
What did you hunt?
Was it rabbits, squirrel, grouse, wild turkey?
Did you ever hunt coons, ground hogs, opossum or deer?
Did you ever gather nuts? What kind?
Did you ever hunt for papaws?
What are they?
Did you gather bittersweet?
What did you do with it?

Did you ever go into the woods and cut fence posts?
What type of saw did you use?
Did you ever gather persimmons?
How about wild asparagus or dandelion greens?
Did you ever gather strawberries along the railroad tracks?

30

TEDDY ROOSEVELT

Do you remember Teddy Roosevelt?
What did he look like?
Was he fat?
Did he wear glasses? What kind?
What did he like to do for fun?
Did he hunt? Where?
Do you remember him being a "rough rider"?
What hill did he lead his soldiers up?
How did he become president?
Did he take over when President McKinley was shot?
Can you think of any big accomplishment during his term in office?
Was he responsible for getting the Panama Canal built?
Was he ever shot? (Yes. Once a bullet pierced his chest. He coughed
     and saw there was no blood so he figured it hadn't hit his lung.
     He went on to speak for an hour.)
What was his daughter's name?
Was it Alice?
Was she a handful?
What were some of the things she did while in the White House? (She
     slid down banisters in front of dignitaries and carried a live garter
     snake in her purse.)
Do you remember him settling the coal miner's strike by threatening
     to send in the national guard?
Did he ever say something you remember?

Did he say, "Walk softly and carry a big stick"?
Was he a good president?

31

BURMA SHAVE SIGNS

Do you remember the signs that used to line the sides of the roads
    called *Burma Shave* signs?
Were they single signs or several signs that gave a continuing message?
Did you enjoy reading those signs?
When did you last see them?
What was *Burma Shave?*
Did you ever use it?
Was it a good product?
Do you remember the messages on the signs?
Were they like these?
> *Passing cars when you can't see, will get you a glimpse of eternity.*
> *When you've made Grandpa look so youthful, his pension board thinks he's untruthful?*
> *She kissed the hairbrush by mistake, she thought it was her husband Jake.*
> *To steal a kiss, he had the knack, but lacked the cheek to get one back.*
> *The boy who gets his girl's applause, must act, not look like Santa Claus.*
> *Road was slippery, curve was sharp, white robe, halo, wings and harp.*
> *Don't pass cars on a curve or hill. If the cops don't get you, the morticians will.*
> *A peach looks good with lots of fuzz, but a man's no peach, and never was.*
> *Dewhiskered kisses frost the misses.*
> *A scratchy chin, like pink socks, puts any romance on the rocks.*

Beneath this stone lies Elmer Gush, tickled to death by his
  shaving brush.
Old McDonald on the farm, shaved so hard he broke his arm.
  Then he bought Burma Shave.

32

TOYS AND GAMES WE'VE LOVED

Did you ever unwind old socks and wrap the yarn to make a ball?
Remember how a mixture of wool and cotton made the best ball?
Remember just picking up a stick to use as a bat?
Did you ever make a whistle?
Did you ever use river cane for it?
Did you ever just bend a piece of tin and poke two holes in it with a
  nail?
Did you ever make a town from pasteboard boxes?
Did you collect scrap wood to make building blocks?
Did you ever cut clowns and puppets from the backs of cereal boxes?
Did you ever have a push mobile?
What was it like?
What kind of sled did you have?
Did you ever just slide on a lard can lid?
Did your father ever make you windmills?
Did you ever make a *rattlebones* to pull across someone's window on
  Halloween night?
Did you ever have a scooter, ice skates, teddy bear, or a rag doll?
Do you remember making a *Jacob's ladder* from a piece of string?
Could you still do that?
Did you have a china head doll or a train?
What games did you play?
Was it *kick the can, harem-scar'em, tinklin-tanklin-Roman buck* or
  run sheep run?

Page 39

How about *Andy Andy over, tally-o, mumble peg* or *crack the whip?*
Were your childhood days good days?
Would you like to live them over again?

Page 40

THE CIRCUS

Did you ever go to the circus?
Did you ever watch the circus train unload?
What animals did the heavy work?
Were they the elephants?
What did they do?
Did they help set up the tents?
What other animals did you see?
Were any of them scary?
Do you know where the circus originated?
Was it from the Romans who pitted beast against beast, and beast
    against man?
In the 1800's how did the circus travel?
Was it by riverboat?
How did it travel when you were young?
Was it by train?
What were some of the acts you saw?
Do you remember any famous clown from long ago?
How about Emmett Kelly?
Do you remember any sayings that originated with the circus?
How about these?

> *Step right up.*
> *Get the show on the road.*
> *Hold your horses.*
> *Come rain or shine.*
> *Jumbo.*

Where was the circus held in your town?
What treats could you buy there?
Was it peppermint sticks and licorice?
Was it popcorn, peanuts and lemonade?
Would you like to go to the circus today?

34

IMMIGRATION

Were you or your parents or grandparents immigrants?

What country did you or they come from?

Where did you or they first arrive when coming to this country?

Was it at Ellis Island?

What was the island like?

Was it scary and foreboding?

Were there rats there?

Did suicides take place there?

Did you or they have to stand in long lines amid what seemed like miles of white rails?

Did you or they have a tag pinned to your shirt with your country of origin?

Did you or they have to go through processing?

How long did that take?

Did a doctor have to check you or them over?

Did people ever get sent back to their country of origin?

Did the captain of the ship that brought them have to pay their way?

Where did you or they go when you left the island?

Was it over to New York?

Did you or they first go to the lower east side of New York?

Did you or they work as peddlers, or in sweat shops, or as shop keepers?

Did you or they then work up to leaving--first to the Bronx, then Brooklyn, and finally out of town?

Do you have any stories about you or your parent's or grandparent's immigration to America?

35

SWEET NOTHINGS

Remember when you'd wile away a Sunday afternoon whipping up a
    big batch of chocolate fudge?

Remember how the saliva glands worked overtime as it cooked?

Did you ever make peanut brittle?

Do you know how peanut brittle was discovered? (It was by accident
    when a preoccupied homemaker was making peanut taffy and
    accidentally put baking soda in her candy instead of cream of
    tartar?)

Did you know fudge was first made as a mistake? (It was meant to be
    a batch of caramels but something went wrong.)

What other kinds of candy have you made?

Did you ever make sassafras taffy and white fudge?
    Did you make any special ones at Christmas time?

Did you pick your own walnuts for the candy?

Do you still like to eat candy?

What's your favorite kind?

36

SIGHTS AND SOUNDS OF LONG AGO

Can you remember some of the sounds of long ago?

How about a rooster crowing?

How about the milkman rattling the bottles on the porch?

Remember the poker being scraped across the grate of the old stove?

Remember the rumble of ashes being shaken down and the sparkling
    kindling being laid in it?

Remember the damper slamming open?

Remember the sound of the coal shovel being scraped across the floor
when the stove or furnace was being fueled?
Remember the clanging and banging of radiators?
Remember the kindling flickering in the kitchen stove?
Remember smelling the biscuits baking?
Remember getting dressed in front of that old stove?
Remember hearing a Model T horn in the distance--"Uga, uga?"

37

THE FIRST TIME YOU SAW AN AUTOMOBILE

Do you remember the first time you saw an automobile?
What did it look like?
How did it sound?
Did you ride in it?
What did the horn sound like?
What were acetylene lights?
Did they blink when you went up a hill? Why?
What color was the car?
Did it have a top on it?
What size tires were on it?
Were they like today's tires, or were they hard rubber?
How much did those early cars cost?
What kind was your first car?
When did you buy it?

DRIVING IN THE OLD DAYS

When you first started driving what was the speed limit?

Remember when it was 10 mph?

Remember when, in town, it was just 8 miles per hour?

Did you need a driver's license when you first drove?

Did you need a car license plate?

What kind of plate was it?

Was it painted on the side of the car?

Was it a little tag that hung inside the car?

Were they ever homemade plates or were they always standard?

How much did a license plate cost?

Do you remember when the first coast-to-coast highway came into being? (1927)

What was the speed limit on that highway? (40 miles per hour)

Was gasoline ever limited?

How much did gasoline cost in those early days?

Tell me about your first car?

Tell me about the first trip you ever took?

Did you have any flat tires?

39

THE OLD TELEPHONE

What was your telephone number long ago?
Was it a seven-digit number or two long rings and a short one, or some
    such combination?
What did your telephone look like?
Did it have a crank on the side?
How did you call a neighbor?
Who was "central"?
Did the phone ring in your house when it wasn't your call?
Did you ever eavesdrop?
Did the operator ever give a general ring?
Did she tell you what movie would be playing?
Did she pass important messages like the ending of the war or election
    reports?

40

SHOPPING AT HOME

Remember the *Raleigh* man?
How about the *Fuller Brush* man?
Did he come to your house?
What did he sell?
Was it brooms, spices, food coloring? What else?
Did many peddlers come by?
Did they have a wagon?
Did it have a scale on it?
Did they ever carry live chickens?
Did they ever carry fabric?
Did you buy much from traveling salesmen? Why?

41

RADIO DAYS

Did you have a radio when you were young?
What did it look like?
Did you ever make a receiver with an oatmeal box and wire?
Remember the one-tube set?
What were some of the old programs?
Who were the sponsors of those programs?
How many channels could you get?
Could you ever hear the Air Force talking?
Who was the *Arkansas Wood Chopper?*
Who was *Lady Dickens?*
Remember *Lullabelle and Scotty?*
Did you ever listen to *Inner Sanctum?*
Was it scary?
Remember *The Shadow Knows?*
Remember *Ma Perkins, Jack Benny* and *Amos* and *Andy?*
Remember hearing the Dorsey brothers playing music?
Do you have a radio today?

42

ELECTRICITY

Can you remember when you first had your house wired for electricity?

How much did it cost? ($13?)

What did that wiring consist of?

Was it just a single wire and socket hanging from the ceiling?

Did you ever unscrew the light bulb and take it to the next room with you?

What kind of lamps did you use before electricity?

Were people ever afraid of electricity in their homes?

What was the first electric appliance you purchased?

Do you remember going to the Public Service and getting free light bulbs?

43

THE GREAT DEPRESSION

Do you remember the Great Depression?

Tell me about it.

What started it?

Do you remember the stock market crash of 1929?

Did you lose any money from a closed bank?

Did you ever see a soup line?

Did farmers manage better than city people?

What happened to the price of crops?

Why were animals slaughtered and milk dumped?

What was the WPA?

What did they do?

Did you ever work for it?

What president started it?

What was the CCC?
What was the PWA?
What was the Hoover house? (outhouse)

44

BIG BANDS

Remember the city bands?
Did your town have one?
Remember 4th of July band concerts?
What was swing music?
Who was Guy Lombardo? Benny Goodman? Harry James?
Did you ever hear them play?
What was "cutting the rug"?
Remember Duke Ellington?
Remember *It's a Sin To Tell a Lie?*
Remember *Alexander's Ragtime Band?*
What other songs do you remember?

45

THE BOX SOCIAL

What is a box social?
Did you ever go to one?
Why did you decorate a shoe box?
What went inside that box?
Did you cook your very best food for it?
What happened to the box?
Was it bid upon?
How much money did it bring in?

Was it around $3.00?
Was that a lot of money in those days?
What was the money used for?
What happened to the guy who bought your pretty decorated box?
Was he your date for the evening?
Did you ever get a girl or guy you didn't
    like?
Where were the box socials held?
Was it usually at the church or the school?
Did you look forward to box socials?

46

THRESHING DAYS

Did you ever work in a threshing ring?
Did every man have a special job?
What were some of those jobs?
Where did you go for lunch?
What were you served?
What was the threshing machine like?
What was it like to farm with horses?
Is the threshing machine still used today?
Why not?

47

MAKING DO

Did you ever have to work hard to make ends meet?
What were some of the things you did?
Did your shoe soles ever wear out?

How did you fix them?

What happened to old coats?

Did you ever clean them with gasoline?

How did you save eggs to last all winter? What was *waterglass?*

Was it a solution to keep eggs in?

How did you keep sausage after butchering?

What happened when you got holes in your socks?

How many dresses or pairs of pants did you have for school?

Did you ever smoke just half a cigarette and save the other half for someone else more needy?

Did you ever eat tin bully beef?

Did you ever hop a railroad car?

Did you ever roll your own cigarettes?

Do you remember when corn sold for just three cents a bushel and you had to sell a whole truck of hogs for just $75?

Do you remember when you didn't have any coffee and how you scorched corn in a pan to make a drink similar to coffee?

Do you remember when you couldn't get sugar?

When was that?

Do you remember when you couldn't buy white flour and had to settle for oatmeal, corn or rye?

Did you learn anything from those tough times?

48

HOSPITALS

Did you ever go to a hospital?

Did you know someone who did?

How much did it cost in the '20's?

What was your room like?

Do you remember when there were gas lights in the operating room?

Who took care of you there?

Why did you have to go?
Did people think hospitals were a place to die?

49

PRESERVING SUMMER'S BOUNTY

How did you cold-pack?
How did you keep carrots and apples for the winter?
Some had root cellars. What if you didn't?
Did you ever dry food?
What was sunshine jam?
Did you ever dry fruit on the roof of your house?
How did you preserve rabbit?
How was apple butter made?
What about cider? sauerkraut?
Did you ever hunt wild asparagus or strawberries along the railroad
    tracks?
Do you remember the old *Presto* steam canner?
Did you ever can outside with the wash boiler?

50

OLD-TIME BARBER SHOPS

Long ago where did you get your hair cut?
Did women ever come to the barber shop for a cut?
What kind of a cut did they get?
Was there a shoe-shine boy at your shop?
How much did a cut cost?
Remember the straight razor?
What is *Bay Rum?*

What does it smell like?
Did your barbers ever do a little singing?
What magazines did you read there?
What color was the striped pole outside the shop?

THE OLD KITCHEN STOVE

Remember the old kitchen stove?
What did it look like?
What was the brand name of it?
Did it have a temperature-controlled oven?
How did you know when cakes were done?
What were warming ovens?
How did you heat the stove?
Where was the wood box kept? the coal bucket?
Did you have a 20-gallon reservoir in the stove?
Did you ever dress for school in front of it?
Did you ever empty the ashes?
What was blacking the old stove?
Why did that have to be done?
What was the brand name of your stove?

Page 54

52

BARN DANCES

Did you ever go to a barn dance?
What were they like?
What did the people sit on?
Was it bales of hay or straw?
Where did the caller stand?
What were the calls?
What were some of the popular songs?
How many squares of dancers were there?
Did you have refreshments?
How did you find out about the dances?
Were they ever held in the hay mow?
What kind of instruments were played?
Was it a fiddle, a harmonica and a guitar?
After barn dances went out, did you roll up the rugs and go
    inside to dance?
Were those good times?

53

HOUSEKEEPING

What did you use to polish furniture?
How was wallpaper cleaned?
Did you cook up a substance using cornmeal, and then rub it on the
    walls like an eraser?
What did you iron with?
What was a fluting iron?
What were the washboards made of?
What was used to scrub the floor? the outhouse?

How were washed curtains hung to dry to avoid shrinking?

Was a curtain stretcher used?

What did it look like?

What kind of a mop did you use?

Was it ever just old clothes?

How did you clean the carpet before vacuum cleaners?

What did you use to clean the old outhouse?

What did you use to scrub the kitchen floor?

What did you use to clean mirrors?

Did you enjoy housekeeping?

SHIRLEY TEMPLE

Who was Shirley Temple?
When was she popular?
Did she ever make a movie?
What were some of them?
What was there about Shirley Temple that mothers tried to copy?
Why did they like her curls?
Was there ever a doll made to look like her?
Did you ever see or buy one?

FOOTBALL LONG AGO

Did you ever play football long ago?
Did you ever see a college team play football?
What was the ball like?
Was the game different than today's?
In what way?
Was it a much rougher game?
Wasn't it a bloodthirsty game of mutilation?
Remember how there were no written rules?
Remember how anyone could play just by signing up?
Remember how you might have to sacrifice your very life if you signed
    up to play?
What were some of the early college teams?
Were they Yale, Princeton, Purdue and Butler?
What year was American football born? (1869)
What kind of uniforms did players wear?

Was it just canvas pants, pillow ticking shirts, tam hats and old shoes with leather strips attached to the bottom for traction?

How did they protect themselves from being bumped too badly?

Did they have their girl friends or mothers sew couch pillows in their uniforms for padding?

How much did those early uniforms cost? (25 cents)

How much do you think today's cost? ($600)

Remember how football was basically a running game?

Remember how a line would form with the players standing bolt up right?

Remember when the ball snapped into play, the opposing team would come into contact with the team standing and they would fall backward like tin soldiers.

Can you remember the big train wreck of 1903 in Indianapolis, Indiana that killed most of the Purdue football team?

56

THE EMPIRE STATE BUILDING

Have you ever been to the Empire State Building?

Did you go all the way to the top?

Was it scary looking down?

How many stories are there in the Empire State Building? (102)

Do you know when it was built?

Wasn't it in the midst of the worst depression ever in 1929?

During the Great Depression, do you know that the building barely sustained itself.

Do you know that someone was hired just to go through and turn the lights on so the building would appear occupied?

Do you remember that depression?

Was it then the tallest building in New York?

Is it today?

How many windows do you think are in that building? (6500)

How often do you think they get washed? (every two weeks)
Would you like to go to the Empire State Building today?
What else would you like to see in New York?

57

HOME COOKING

Remember the good home cooking of long ago?
Do you miss some of those specialties today? Which ones?
What did you used to eat for breakfast?
What kind of meat was served?
Did you have fresh hot biscuits?
What did you serve on the biscuits?
Was it sizzling hot gravy or sorghum molasses or your very
    special jam?
What kind of jam and jelly did you make?
Did you ever have spiced tomato preserves?
Did you use fruit pectin?
Did you ever make apple butter out over the open fire?
Did you ever make cornmeal mush?
How did you do it?
Did you start it the night before?
What about homemade butter?
Did you have it?
Did you ever eat rolled oats and fried muffins?
When someone was sick, did you serve them milk toast?
What was that?
How about coffee toast?
Remember potato soup with drop noodles?
Did you make pickles in big crocks?
What kind?
How did you do it?
What were your favorite cookies to make?

Page 59

Were they raisin, sugar, or molasses cookies?
Did you often have pineapple upside down cake or jelly cake?
What is jelly cake?
Would you like to have some of those goodies today?

SCHOOL DAYS, GOLDEN RULE DAYS

Can you remember your early school days?
How did you get to school?
Did you ride in a school hack?
Did you walk? How far?
What about when there was lots of snow on the ground?
What did you wear?
Where did you hang your coats and put your overshoes?
Where did you get a drink?
What was your teacher's name?
Did you like her?
Why or why not?
What did you play at recess?
Did you have a back house out behind the school?
Did you ever get switched?
How else did the teacher punish kids?
Did they have to wear dunce caps?
Did they have to put their nose in a circle on the board?
Did you even have black boards?
What did you use to write your work on?
Was it a slate board?
How were the big blackboards attached to the walls?
Was it with ropes?
What subjects did you learn?
How far did you go in school?
Did you use the *McGuffey Reader* and *Olney's Geography?*
Did you use *Kirkham's Grammar* and *Webster's English Speller?*
Do you remember "borrowing one" and "singing geography" where
    you learned states and capitals, rivers and mountains through
    sing-song recitation?
Did you like school?
Would you like to visit a school today?

Page 63

59

PLASTIC

Did you have plastic when you were young?

What were your dishes made of?

Was it granite, porcelain or aluminum?

When do you think plastic first came in?

Would you believe it has been around in a form for centuries?

Did you know the first plastic type product came from animal hoofs and horns?

Remember the celluloid collars?

Weren't they a form of plastic? (Toys, photo film, cutlery and hand mirrors were also made from celluloid.)

Didn't your bakeware between 1910 and 1941 have plastic handles?

Can you remember when *Rubbermaid* came in, in the 30's?

Wasn't it a wonderful product?

What items were made from it?

Can you remember when *Tupperware* came in around 1945?

60

OTHER OLD HEALTH CARE REMEDIES

Were you ever given quinine?

What for?

Was it for fevers?

Wasn't it also used for malaria?

Do you remember a drink made from cocaine derived from coca leaves, a forerunner of today's Coca Cola?

Can you remember any old tonics?

How about *Lydia Pinkham's* tonic for women, *Triple S.* tonic, *IQS* tonic containing iron, *Black Draught, Hadacol* and *Geritol?*

Remember how most of these tonics contained a high concentration of alcohol?

Did you ever use sassafras tea as a spring tonic?

Did you ever use baking soda as a stomach ailment?

Do you remember how already chewed tobacco was used?

Was it placed on a wound such as when someone stepped on a nail?

What were turpentine stoops?

Weren't they just a rag dipped in turpentine and water and wrung out and placed on the chest for colds, or on the abdomen for gas or bowel obstruction?

Did you ever use kerosene for chiggers?

Did you ever place a piece of steak over a black eye?

What was camphor oil used for?

Wasn't it mixed with alcohol and inserted in the ear?

Wasn't it also used to swab sore throats?

Do you remember the days before penicillin?

Remember the heart/lung machine?

Did you use any of these old remedies?

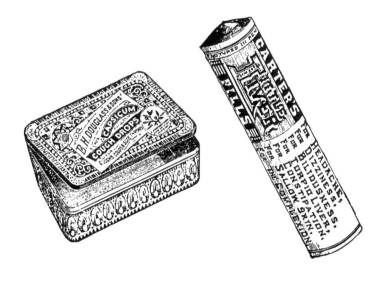

61

THE OLD FAMILY DOCTOR

Do you remember your family doctor?
What was his name?
Did he ever come to your house? Why?
How did he arrive there?
Did he have a Model T or a horse?
Who was sick?
Did he ever do an operation at your house?
Was it on the kitchen table?
Did he ever deliver a baby at your house?
How did you pay him?
Did you ever pay him with anything other than money?
What medicines did he tell you to take?
Did he ever send you to the hospital?
Did you ever visit his office?
What did it look like?
What medicines did he give you?
What for?
Did you get shots then?
Did he ever give you any candy or special treats?
Does your doctor today seem like the old family doc?

LIBERATION FOR WOMEN

Can you remember when women began to get more freedom?
Was it in the '20's?
Do you remember the first time you voted?
Do you remember when hemlines began to rise?
Did you ever wear your dresses at ankle length?
What was the hemline in the '20's?
Did women begin to smoke in the '20's?
Did you ever try it?
Did you know any women who did?
Did you read fashion magazines then?
What did men think of this new freedom for women?
Did you begin to wear make-up at this time?
Did you hold a job outside the home?
What caused women to first seek jobs?
Was it the two world wars?
What type of jobs did women hold?
Did you like having your own money?
Did you discard your corset in the '20's?
When did you quit wearing hats regularly?
Were you aware that women's roles were changing then?

63

THE ICE MAN

Do you remember the ice man?
How did he dress?
What transportation did he have?
How did he break the ice from the huge block?

Did he use a big pick?

How did he carry the big block into your house?

Where did he put it in the house?

What did the sign mean that you hung in the window reading 10, 25, or 50?

Was that the pounds of ice you wanted?

Did you ever follow the ice man looking for ice chips?

Did you ever want to be an ice man?

Do you remember the old ice house?

Where was it located?

Did you ever go there?

Did your father ever go to the river and cut ice?

DEATH IN THE OLD DAYS

As a child, do you remember someone dying? Who?

Do you remember when wakes where held at home?

Did you ever go to any?

Did someone always stay up all night with the body?

Were mirrors ever covered? Why?

Were clocks stopped? Why?

Were pennies ever put on the eyes of the deceased? Why?

Did you ever help take care of someone who died?

Were you afraid of death as a child?

Are you now? Why?

Did you ever know someone who dug up their dead when they moved
  and took them with them?

Did you ever hear that people's hair and fingernails continue to grow
  after they have been buried?

Did you ever go to the cemetery to look at tombstones?

Do you enjoy looking at all the old names?

Do you ever wonder what it will be like to die?

Do you believe Jesus has a better life prepared for you if you repent,
  believe He died for your sins, and trust Him to save you?

OLD-FASHIONED CHRISTMAS

Remember Christmas long ago?
Was it different than today? How?
Were the toys received different from today's?
What was the most favorite toy you ever received?
Was it a teddy bear, a china doll, a wagon or a sled?
Did you ever *not* get any presents at Christmas?
Did you ever just receive an orange for Christmas?
What kind of candy did you receive?
Were gifts often homemade?
How did you spend Christmas?
Did you go to church?
Did you have company, or did you travel elsewhere?
What kind of a Christmas tree did you have?
Did you go to the woods for it?
How did you decorate it?
Did you ever make paper chains and ornaments?
Did it have candles on it?
What kind?
When were they lit?
Was it ever put up prior to Christmas eve?
Did you hang stockings? Where?
What would be put in them?
What foods did you eat?
Did you ever have persimmon pudding? plum pudding?
Did you ever help pluck the goose?
Did you make tallow candles?
Did you sing songs? Which ones?
Did you go sleigh riding?
Was Christmas more fun then than now?

BASKET, BASKET

Do you remember using lots of baskets long ago?
What did you use them for?
Did you take one shopping with you?
What kind?
What was your clothes basket like?
Did you keep bread in a basket?
Did you have a picnic basket?
What did you keep your sewing in?
What kind of basket was used for early basketball?
Was it a peach basket?
Do you remember any other kinds of baskets you used?
Do you still like baskets?

67

ELECTIONS

Remember voting long ago?
Remember election day and how presidents were discussed?
Where did you vote?
How did you find out who won the election?
Did you ever go to your newspaper office and wait outside for them to
    hold signs out the windows which gave election news?
Did "central," on the telephone, ring you with election reports?
How did you vote?
Did you use paper ballots?
Was there cheating?
Who was your favorite president?
Do you think it's important to vote?
Do you vote today?

68

THE LAMPLIGHTER

Do you remember the lamplighter?
What was his job?
What did he carry with him?
Was it a ladder?
What did he use it for?
Was it to climb up the lamp post?
He came around twice a day. Why?
Didn't he light the lamp in the evening and put it out in the morning?
What else do you remember about the lamplighter?

69

OLD CARS

What kind of car was your first one?

Was it a *Model T?*

What did it look like?

Do you remember other kinds of cars?

What car was called the bootleggers favorite?

Was it the *Stutz Bearcat* with the tall shiny radiator?

Do you remember the *Haynes* whose body was made by buggy makers and had 17 coats of paint?

Do you remember when Indianapolis was like automobile city?

Wasn't that before Detroit became the auto capitol?

What was the *Morman* like?

Was it used by bootleggers?

Remember the *Franklin* with a wooden frame?

How about the *Peerless* and the *Saxon?*

Wasn't the *Saxon* a light car like a bicycle?

Do you remember the *Whippet* made in Toledo by Overland?

Do you remember the *Moon,* assembled in Elkart, Indiana?

Remember how it had a big nickel-plated radiator and resembled a *Rolls Royce?*

Remember the *Hupmobile?*

Remember how it had a little tank on the side and how you lit a match and turned a key and the acetylene gas ignited to create a light?

Remember the straps on the *Hupmobile* to hold the top down?

Can you remember the *Stanley Steamer?*

What was it like?

Did it take a while to start?

Do you remember the little burner on the back where you had to throw coal in to work up steam?

Remember how after you once got it started, you could pull back on the throttle and throw gravel?

Are today's cars like those old ones?

Page 75

THE GREAT CHICAGO FIRE

Did your parents or grandparents ever talk about the great Chicago fire?

When did it take place?

Was it 1871?

How did the fire start?

What was the lady's name who owned the cow who started it?

Was it Mrs. O'Leary?

Do you know how many died? (120 bodies were recovered, but the death toll may have been as high as 300.)

Do you know who was president then?

Wasn't it Ulysses S. Grant?

What kind of fire equipment was used?

Wasn't it hand pumpers that looked like toys against the giant flames?

How do you think they fought the Chicago fire?

Do you think they watered down roofs?

Do you think they used dynamite to blow up some buildings hoping to halt the path of flames?

Where do you think people went to escape the flames?

Do you think they got in the middle of the river or lake?

Do you think fire skipped across bridges?

Did you know that the sky was invisible due to the smoke?

Do you think people panicked?

Would you have?

Where would you have gone for safety?

Were you ever in a fire?

Do you know how long the Chicago fire burned?

Wasn't it all day and all night?

Do you know why it finally stopped?

Would you believe it rained?

What do you think happened in Chicago after the fire?

Do you think relief centers were set up to help?

71

DRUMMERS

What was a drummer?

Wasn't it someone other than one who played the drum?

Was he like a traveling salesman?

How did he travel?

Wasn't it on horseback?

Remember how he would rent a horse and ride to the next town and change horses at the livery stable?

What wares did he peddle?

Did some carry eye glasses, and you tried them on until you found one that felt comfortable?

Did some peddle cloth, needles, thread and thimbles?

Remember how fabric was often hard to come by?

Did some carry pots and pans?

Did you ever know an Indian drummer who peddled liniment called *White Owl* and also horse liniment?

Remember the scissor's sharpener?

Did he ever come to your house?

How did he sharpen your scissors?

How would a drummer attract attention when he came to town?

Did he often put on a show by playing an instrument?

72

GRANDMA AND GRANDPA

Do you remember your grandparents?

What did they look like?

How did Grandma wear her hair?

Was it in a little knot on the back of her head?

Did she wear braids?
Was she fat or skinny?
Was she stern or friendly?
Did you like to visit her?
Did she bake you good treats?
What were they?
What about Grandpa?
What did he look like?
Did he wear suspenders?
Did he wear a beard or a mustache?
Was he fat or thin?
Was he a farmer or did he work in the city?
Was he good natured? a grouch?
Did he smoke?
What was his house like?
How often did you visit?
Are you a grandparent today?
Do you enjoy the role of grandparent?

73

THE OLD COUNTRY STORE

Remember the old country store?
What did it look like?
Was food stored in big barrels?
What was in the barrels?
Was it flour, sugar, pickles, corn meal, peanut butter and peanuts?
What else?
What did the store cases look like?
Were they wooden?
Did the store keeper sell candy?
What kind?
Did you like to go to the store?

Do you remember *Arbuckle* sugar and *Silver Moon* flour?
What type of laundry soap did you buy?
Was it *Star City* and *P and G?*
Did you put your groceries on the bill rather than paying cash?
Was there any fringe benefit when you paid your bill?
Didn't you get a free sack of candy when it was paid?
How did you carry your groceries home?
Were paper bags used then?
Where was your old store located?
Is it still there?
Did you buy animal feed there?
Did it come in cotton print sacks?
What did you do with that print fabric?
Was there a cracker barrel at your store?
Did the cat ever sleep on the crackers?

74

WE REMEMBER THE SLAVES

Did you ever know any former slaves?
Did your parents ever talk about any of them?
What were their names?
Did any of them have beating marks still on their bodies?
Were any of them rebellious?
What do you think made them rebellious?
Do you know of any underground railroads that helped slaves escape?
What president freed the slaves?
What do you think about slavery?
Was it a bad thing?

GRANDMA'S BEAUTY SECRETS

Do you still like to look pretty?
Do you remember back before make-up was popular?
What did you use for rouge?
Did you ever wet red tissue paper, mesh vegetable bags or a flag
and rub them on your cheeks for color?
What did you use for powder before makeup was popular?
Did you ever use flour, cornstarch or talc on your face?
Didn't you look really white?
How did you keep your hair nice?
Did you use rain water on it?
How did you roll it?
Did you use rags for curlers?
Did you ever use milk or vinegar on your hair?
Did you use a curling iron?
Before electricity, how did you heat the curling iron?
Did you put it down the lamp flue?
Did you ever use mayonnaise for face cream?
How about sweet cream?
What did you use to clean your teeth before toothpaste?
Was it salt or soda?
Did women worry about diets back then, or was it fashionable to be
a little heavier?

Page 80

Page 81

76

FIRE FIGHTING LONG AGO

Did you ever belong to the fire department?
Do you remember seeing any fires long ago?
What is a bucket brigade?
Did you ever take part in one?
Were they effective?
Were there many barn fires long ago?
Did you ever see a hand pumper?
Remember that old fire engine that was a wooden wagon with a brass
     topped canister to carry the water?
Remember how four fast horses pulled it through the town?
Remember how children came out to watch the excitement?
Did you ever visit the old fire station?
Did the firemen have a fire pole to slide down?
How are today's fire engines different than the old ones?

77

GANGSTERS

Do you remember any gangsters in your town long ago?
Do you remember the bank robbers of the '30's?
Did you ever see a bank robber?
Were you afraid of them?
What is a "protection" tax?
Did bank robbers make businesses pay these so they wouldn't get
     robbed?
Did your National Guard ever train men to fight bank robbers?
Do you know of any banks getting robbed?
Did you lose any money then?

CHURCH OF MY CHILDHOOD

Do you remember the first church you attended?
Was it a large church or a small one?
Do you remember the minister or priest?
What color was that church?
Was it in town or the country?
Did it have a tall steeple?
Was it brick or wood?
Did you know many people there?
Did they get along well?
What did you wear to church?
Did women wear hats?
What music was played?
What songs did you sing?
Do you like to go to church today?
How is church different today than in your childhood?

THE OLD JAIL

Do you have a jail in your town?
Is it the same one that was there when you were a child?
Did you ever visit that jail?
What was it like?
Was it fearsome?
Did a sheriff stay there all the time?
What type of prisoners were there?
Was it a large jail or a small one?
What is a turnkey?

How long a shift did he work?

Did he work 24 hours on and 24 hours off?

Did you ever visit a big prison?

How do you think today's prisons are different from the old-time
jail?

80

COME FLY WITH ME

Can you remember the first time you saw an airplane?

Did it scare you?

Did you wonder what it was?

Was it noisy?

Did you ever get to ride in one?

Was there an airport in your town?

What was it called?

Did you ever go to an air show?

What took place there?

Did you ever know a pilot?

Do you remember the Lindbergh flight?

Do you remember Amelia Earhart's flight?

Would you like to fly today?

SECTION 5

81

THE DAY THE BANKS CLOSED

Do you remember the day the banks closed their doors for business?

Do you remember how the Great Depression began?

Do you remember the big stock market crash?

What year was that?

Was it 1929?

Remember people being lined up for a whole block outside the bank trying to get their own money out?

Do you remember people going down to the bank every day trying to get some of their money out?

Remember how no one trusted banks for a while?

Did you?

Where did you keep your money after the banks closed?

Did you ever hide it in the bedpost, in an old chair, under the rug or in a book?

Did you ever forget where you put it?

When the banks reopened, did you get all your money back or just a portion?

How did you start trusting them again?

What was your bank called?

What were some of the other banks in your town?

Do you remember your banker's name?
Do you trust banks today?
Do you think they could fail again?

82

BUTCHERING DAY

Do you remember butchering day long ago?
Was it a day that was looked forward to?
When butchering had to be done, who helped?
Did friends and neighbors come for the day?
What was the first thing you had to do?
Did you begin by shooting the animal and bleeding it?
What was the next step?
Did you dip it in hot water and scrape off the hair?
What next?
Was the hog or animal thrown over someone's shoulder and rolled onto a large table where it was cut and had its intestines and other organs removed?
Was some of the meat smoked?
Which parts?
What was your recipe for sugar curing?
Was it something like this--1/2 cup salt, 1 cup brown sugar, and 1 teaspoon of red pepper?
Before refrigeration, how did you keep the meat from spoiling?
Did you fry it down and pack it in big crocks covered with fat?
Where did you store this crock?
Was it in the cool cellar?
Did you can any of the meat and seal it with a rubber seal?
How many men helped work on butchering?
What did the women do while the men worked?
Were they in the house making head cheese?
What is head cheese?

Page 86

Did you, as a child, ever skip school on butchering day?
Did you pretend to be sick, but then make a remarkable recovery?
What part of the animal did the kids stand around and wait for?
Was it the bladder so they could play with it like a balloon?
Were their any jobs especially for women?
Did they usually clean the intestines?
Who made the lard?
Did the women stand around and nag the men, "Don't burn it!
    Don't burn it!"
Where did cracklings come from?
Were they big chunks of fat that were fried down?
Were kids eager to eat these?
Did farmers leave the butchering to go home and do their own chores
    and then return?
When evening came, did everyone go inside?
What did they have to eat?
Was it a fresh fried sausage sandwich?

SUPERSTITION

Were you ever superstitious?

Did you ever carry a rabbit's foot?

How about a buckeye in your pocket?

Did you ever hunt for a four leaf clover? Why?

Ever wonder where superstitions came from?

Have you ever been afraid to walk under a ladder?

Did you know *that* superstition originated in Asia centuries ago when criminals were hung from the seventh rung of a ladder. Death was thought to be contagious.

Did you ever say "knock on wood"?

Do you know that originated long ago when folks would knock on a tree seeking to get the tree god to grant them a favor?

Ever wonder why June seems to be the month of brides? (It was because in Roman mythology, Juno, the goddess of women, was supposed to have blessed weddings in her month.)

Why is rice thrown at weddings? (supposedly to appease evil spirits and provide many children)

Did you ever break a wishbone of the chicken? Why?

Do you know *that* started 2500 years ago when people dried chicken collar bones in the sun. Then people with a need touched them and asked the gods a favor?

Did you ever hesitate to cross the path of a black cat?

Do you know that originated in the middle ages when cats were the companions of witches and it was thought that after seven years the cat would turn into a witch?

Ever wonder why people say "God bless you" when you sneeze (People believed evil spirits jumped out with the sneeze and felt the saying provided protection.)

Did you ever throw a pinch of salt over your left shoulder? (This was done to bribe harmful spirits, and as a means of protection.)

Are you superstitious today?
Did you know there is no need to be?

84

GONE FISHING

Remember those long, lazy days curled up on the bank of the old creek
with fishing pole in hand?
What did you use for a fishing pole?
Was it ever just a stick with a string tied on it?
Did you ever have to wade out into the deep for a bite on your line?
Where was your favorite fishing hole?
How many fish did you catch at one time?
What was the biggest you ever caught?
Did you ever use a throw line?
What was that?
Did you ever snare fish with a loop of copper wire which was soft and
bendable? When the fish got in the loop, did he give a quick jerk?
Did you ever gig catfish?
Was there a special knack to using a cane pole?
When you got a bite, did you quickly throw your pole around and
land the fish on the bank?
Did you ever get your line tangled in tree branches?
Who first took you fishing?
What did you use for bait?
Was it grub worms or red worms?
Did you ever use cornmeal and make balls by boiling them?
Did you ever use chicken livers?
Who cleaned the fish you caught?
Would you like to go fishing today?
What is your very best fish story?

WASHDAY

Did you ever scrub on an old washboard?
What was the washboard made of?
Was it zinc, glass or copper?
How big was it?
Can you show us the motion you used on it?
How long did it take to do the wash?
What kind of soap did you use?
Did you use lye soap?
Did you ever make your own soap?
How did you heat the water?
Did your hands ever get tired of wringing out clothes?
Do you remember when you got your first wringer?
Do you remember when you got your first electric washing machine?
As a child, did you ever have to pull the handle of the washing
machine back and forth to agitate the wet clothes?
Did you dread wash day as a child?
What food was usually served on wash day?
Was it beans?
Is that why they were called "wash beans"?

86

OLD-TIME SONGS

Do you like to sing?
Did you sing long ago?
Did you ever sing at church?
Did you sing in a choir or solo?
What was your favorite song when you were young?
Can you sing it today?
Do you like today's music?
What decade had the best music?
Did you like the big band era?
Did you like the roaring '20's music?
Do you remember *Daisy Daisy*?
Can you sing a little of it?
Do you remember *Sleepy Time Gal*?
How about *Little Brown Jug* or *Yes Sir That's My Baby*?
Do you remember *I Want a Girl Just Like the Girl Who Married Dear Old Dad*?

Can you sing a little of it?

Do you remember *The Old Gray Mare*, *Casey Jones*, *Royal Telephone*, and *Bicycle Built for Two*?

What about *The Wabash Canon Ball and Swinging Down The Lane*?

Do you like it when groups come in to sing?

Would you like to sing along with them?

Would you like an opportunity to sing by yourself before a group?

87

THE OLD DRUG STORE

Do you remember the old drugstore of your childhood?

Where was it located?

Did you go there often?

Did it have a soda fountain?

What did you buy there?

Do you remember your pharmacist's name?

What kinds of medicine did you buy?

How was it packaged?

Were capsules packed in little boxes?

Did ointments come in porcelain jars?

Were powders wrapped in little squares of paper and then packed in a box?

Did you ever buy oil of clove for a tooth ache?

Did you ever buy *Arnica*, a brown liquid for sprains?

Did you use yellowroot for sore throats?

Did you ever purchase quinine and use it in cocoa syrup?

Remember before gum opium was a strict narcotic how you could go to the drugstore and buy a dime or a quarter's worth of it?

Remember how the pharmacist would roll out a little ball and cut a piece off and wrap it in paper?

Was opium used as a pain killer?

Did you ever use it? Was it also used as a stimulant?

What did prescriptions cost long ago?

Could you buy 12 capsules for 50 cents and four ounces of cough syrup for 75 cents?

Is your old drugstore still in operation?

Would you like to visit there again if it was?

88

AILING IN THE OLD DAYS

Do you remember the diseases of long ago?

What was *consumption?*

Was it the same as T.B.?

How was it treated?

Did those with it have to sleep outside all summer and leave the windows open in winter?

What medicines were given?

Was it whiskey and quinine?

What was *infantile paralysis?*

Was it *polio?*

What president had it?

Was it FDR?

What was *diphtheria?*

How did you know you had it?

Was it a very sore throat?

What was *scarlet fever?*

Did the body turn bright red?

What was *typhoid fever?*

Was it a sickness in the bowels?

Did you know people who had to learn to walk all over again because of it?

What was *small pox?*

Did it ever become an epidemic?

How was pneumonia treated?

Were mustard plasters applied to the chest?
Did you ever have German measles?
How were they treated?
What was the itch?
Did it really last seven years?
What did it mean to be quarantined?
Did they really hang a sign on your front door?
What were pest houses?
Were they where people with infectious diseases went?
Did you ever go there?
Did you know anyone who did?
Are you glad medicine is so much better today?

89

THE LONE EAGLE

· Who was the Lone Eagle?
Was it Charles A. Lindbergh?
What major accomplishment did he make?
Was it to be the first solo flyer of the Atlantic?
Do you remember when it happened?
Were you anxiously waiting for news of his arrival in Paris?
Do you know who was president then?
Was it Calvin Coolidge?
What year was this flight?
Was it 1927?
Do you think it began to make people less afraid of flying?
Do you remember anything unusual about his baby son?
Was he kidnapped?
Did they find the man who did it?
Do you think he really did it?
Do you remember the Wright brothers?
Would you like to fly today?

THE WABASH AND ERIE CANAL

Did you ever hear of the *Wabash and Erie* canal?

What was it?

Was it a man dug waterway with one-way traffic?

Were cities actually built with canals bringing in materials?

Weren't canals the transportation that first carried rails for railroads?

Do you know of any other canals?

When were they popular?

Was it in the mid 1800's?

Why did the canals go out of use?

Was it because the railroad came in?

Did your parents ever ride a canal boat?

Did they ever talk about the canals?

What were these boats called?

Were they packets?

Do you remember the cost to ride a packet boat?

Wasn't it about four cents a mile?

Do you know how fast the boats traveled?

Do you think travel on canals was slow?

Wasn't it just four miles per hour?

What was the "tow path?"

Was that land beside the canal where horses walked and pulled the packet boats along?

Did you ever see a tow path?

Have you ever seen the remains of a canal?

PROHIBITION

Do you remember prohibition?
What was it?
Could you buy any liquor then?
What was a bootlegger?
What was a revenue officer?
Did he hunt down bootleggers?
Did you ever know any bootleggers?
Did you ever make home brew during prohibition?
What was "near beer"?
Was it beer with 99% of the alcohol removed?
Was liquor expensive on the black market?
Was it alright to make beer at home?
Could you make it and give it away, or could you just use it for your
        own family?
Did you make beer by beginning with two cans of batter which you
        bought to make five gallons of beer?
Did you have your own bottle capper?
What ingredients were used to make beer?
Did you use yeast and hops?
Did a foam form as it fermented?
How long did it take to make beer?
Did you ever make wine?
Did you, as a child, ever sneak any of your dad's?
Did it make you sick?
Do you remember the names of some home brew?
Have you ever heard of *White Lightening, Mountain Moonlight* and
        White Mule?
Do you think prohibition was a good thing or not?
Do you think we should have it today?

THE MILKMAN

Do you remember the milkman?
What was his name?
What time a day did he deliver the milk?
How did you pay the milkman?
Did you leave the money out in the empty bottles?
Do you remember when the milkman drove a horse-drawn wagon?
What were the milk bottles made out of?
What settled on the top of each fresh bottle of milk?
Was it fresh, rich cream?
Did you like to eat that?
What did the milkman wear?
Was it fresh white overalls?
How did the milkman keep his milk cold?
Did he carry ice on the truck?
Did you ever chase after him to get a piece of ice?
Did you have your own cows rather than a milkman?
How much milk did they give each day?
Do you like to drink milk today?

93

4TH OF JULY

Did you enjoy the 4th of July as a child?
How did you celebrate it?
Did you go to the park?
Did you attend a band concert?
Did you have a picnic?
What did you have to eat?

Was it fried chicken, potato salad, home canned pickles and berry
   pies?
Did you have watermelon for dessert?
What did you drink?
Was it lemonade?
What did you do at the park for fun?
Did you swing?
Did you play horseshoe?
Did you go for a boat ride?
Were there contests and games?
Did the boys ever wrestle a greased pig?
Did they ever try to climb a greased pole?
Did you ever have watermelon-seed-spitting contests?
How far could you spit a seed?
How did the girls dress?
Did they wear dresses to the park?
Did they wear bonnets to protect their complexions?
Did the boys were knee length pants?
Was the 4th of July a very special day?

94

MY FAVORITE PET

Did you ever have a very favorite pet?
What was it?
Was it a dog or a cat?
What was its name?
Did it do anything special?
Did it know any tricks?
What ever happened to your pet?
Tell me all about your favorite pets?
Would you like to have a pet today?

95

THE OLD OUTHOUSE

Did you have an outhouse when you were a kid?

What did it look like?

Was it a one holer or two?

Did it have a special small hole for children?

What did you use for toilet paper?

Was it really the *Sears* catalog?

Was it ever corn cobs?

Whose job was it to clean the outhouse?

What did you clean it with?

Did your mother use her wash water that had lye in it to clean the outdoor toilet?

Did you mind going out there at night?

Did you ever hear an owl while there?

Was it ever too cold to make the trip?

Did the snow ever blow hard and block the door so you couldn't get out?

Did brothers or sisters ever lock you in?

Do you remember the sound of rain pounding when you were in there?

Did you ever use a granite pot inside your house at night?

What ever happened to that back house?

Do you remember when the WPA built nice outhouses with cement bottoms?

Are you glad you do not have to make that trip out back today?

96

SUNDAYS WERE SPECIAL

How did you spend Sunday when you were a child?

Did you go to church?
Did you go visiting?
Where did you go?
Did you visit relatives?
Did you have company?
Did you ever go to the park?
Did you go for long walks?
Did you go in the woods?
Were you allowed to fish on Sunday?
Did you still have to do chores on Sunday?
Were you allowed to work much?
Did you spend time with cousins and friends?
Did you ever make fudge on Sundays?
Did you listen to the radio?
Did you have a big dinner?
What might you have for dinner then?

97

THE PARLOR

Did your house have a parlor?
Was it opened only on Sundays?
Did you like to go in there?
Were you ever allowed to use it to spend time with your date?
What did it look like?
Were there lace curtains?
Were there crocheted doilies and crocheted lace table cloths hanging
    to the floor on tables?
Was there a piano in there?
Did you keep any special photographs there?
Was there a big velvet couch and overstuffed chairs?
What kind of a couch was there?
Do you think today's houses should have parlors?

CLOTHES LONG AGO

Did you have a lot of clothes when you were young?
Did you just have two or three outfits?
Did you ever wear the same outfit to school for several days in a row?
Did you wear hand-me-downs?
Were you embarrassed to do this?
Did you have dress clothes and play clothes?
When dress clothes got old, did they become play clothes?
Did you ever have to go barefoot starting in spring just to save on your
   shoes?
Did you ever have to put cardboard in your shoes to cover the holes
   in the soles?
Did you wear underwear made from feed sacks?
Did your mother ever knit your socks?
What did she do when they got a hole in them?
Were you thankful for the clothes you had then?
Do you think kids today have too many clothes?

AMELIA EARHART

Who was Amelia Earhart?
Do you know what she is famous for?
Do you remember when she attempted her "around the world" flight?
What year was that?
Was it 1937?
What kind of a plane did she use?
Was it a twin-engine Lockheed Electra?

Was she successful on her flight?

What do you think ever happened to her?

Do you think she was a woman's libber before her time?

Do you remember how she wore pants when other women wore only dresses?

Do you remember how she always wore a rolled scarf around her neck?

How did she wear her hair?

Did you ever see her?

Did you know at what university she acted as women's student advisor?

Wasn't it Purdue University in West Lafayette, Indiana?

Did they not provide her with a plane for her flight?

Did you know many of her things are stored at Purdue today?

Do you know what Amelia Earhart's favorite drink was?

Wasn't it buttermilk?

Remember how college kids imitated everything she did?

Did you know she was aviation editor for *Cosmopolitan* magazine?

Did you know she marketed a whole line of jewelry made from airplane parts?

Do you admire Amelia Earhart?

Would you have been as brave as she was?

100

WOMEN'S WORK

Remember long ago how the homemaker organized her week?

Did she always do the same thing on each day?

What was Monday set aside for?

Was it washing?

What was special about Tuesday?

Was it not ironing day?

What about Wednesday?

Do you remember what *you* did on Wednesday?
Was it set aside for visiting the sick and others?
What did you do on Thursday?
Was that sewing day?
Did you mend clothes or make new ones?
And I'm sure you remember what Friday was for.
Wasn't it for doing housecleaning?
What did you do on Saturday?
Was that the day you baked bread, cakes and pies?
What about Sunday?
Did you still have to prepare a big meal?
Did you squeeze other chores in between your regularly scheduled
    ones?
Did you churn butter?
Did you raise, kill, dress and cook chickens?
Did you gather eggs?
Did you ever help with the milking?
Did you keep the old stove full of wood?
Did you chop wood?
Did you tend a garden?
How big was it?
Did you can the produce?
How did you store apples and carrots?
Did you rear a large family while you did all these jobs?
Would you like to go back to those days again today?

TWENTY TIPS FOR LEADING
A LIVELY REMINISCENT GROUP

1) Personally invite residents and tease them a little by hinting at one or two old-days subjects you'll be discussing. Say something like, "I wasn't born yet when most of these things took place, so I need you there because you can probably tell us many things about those days. Won't you please come and help me out?"

2) Try to involve several alert residents who will be the core of the group. Yet, remember to include a few residents who are not generally very responsive. Often, when discussion starts, less responsive residents come out of their shell and join in the conversation.

3) Do not allow staff members to bring unruly or disruptive residents into your group. This quickly upsets alert residents who will become frustrated and leave. Thus your group will quickly end. In a friendly manner, explain this to staff members who insist on bringing these residents into your reminiscent group.

4) Prepare thoroughly for what will be discussed in your group. Use subjects in *Remembering the Good Old Days* or visit your library and find books on this era. One such book series is *This Fabulous Century* put out by Time-Life books. It covers events from the late 1800's through the '50's. Make a list of discussion starters.

5) Collect some visual aids. These stimulate residents to recall the days of their youth. One source is *Ideals*, a picturesque bi-monthly publication put out by Ideals Publishing Company, 11315 Watertown

Plank Road, Milwaukee, Wisconsin 53226. Another good source is Norman Rockwell prints. You may find a book of these at your library.

6) Encourage a few residents each time to bring their photograph albums. These will probably contain some old-time photos sure to spark memories in the others.

7) Serving refreshments is a great incentive for residents to come. Donuts and coffee are a sure bet for morning discussion groups. Just remember to keep some diabetic alternatives handy. For afternoon groups, you might serve punch and cookies, cut raw vegetables, cheese and crackers, or cut up fresh fruit. Cider or juices work well for drinks.

8) Seat yourself or the discussion leader centrally at the table so you can be seen and heard by all residents. If absolutely necessary, use a small hand-held microphone for residents' convenience. This can take some of the spontaneity out of the group.

9) Gather residents close around. If at all possible, use a single table. Extra large groups are not good because some can't hear and consequently won't participate. This halts their return to the group.

10) Begin your group by asking a question about the old days? Explain that you weren't there when this particular happening took place, or when things were done that way. Say you would really like to know more about it.

11) It pays to *play dumb* even when you know the answer, and you well may if you have done your research before the group.

12) It's a wise activity director who takes notes of what's being discussed. First off, residents feel very important to think what they are telling you is worthy of note taking. Second, you have the makings for some great stories for your newsletter. Third, the material can be filed and used for future reminiscent groups. Fourth, you may well uncover a story that will entice the press to come and interview your residents. Some of this material can be used to write your press release that will tempt them to come and get the whole story.

13) Limit your group to no more than one hour. Though residents may seemingly want to talk longer, it's better they go away wanting more than being overly tired. If that happens, next time they may refuse to come.

14) Listen carefully when a resident shares anything. This builds them up and encourages them to share more.

15) Allow only one resident to talk at a time. Gently discourage others from carrying on conversations when another resident is sharing. Explain that you want to hear what *everyone* has to say and that their time will come soon. Do not let this come across as a rebuke, but rather as a sincere desire to hear them out.

16) Warmly thank each resident for coming and for helping you to know about an era you couldn't have known without them. Tell them you can't wait till the next group so you can hear more of their stories.

17) Set a particular day each week for reminiscent group. That way residents can plan for it. You might, for their sake, just call it "coffee and donuts" or "refreshment time" rather than "discussion group." Mornings may be preferable to afternoons, because reminiscing is a pick-me-up. It can help residents be more alert the rest of the day.

18) Don't limit reminiscing to a group activity. Take the subjects you've discussed at your group to bedside residents and let them recall those days. Use it for a one on one activity when you meet residents in the hall, or for small groups of residents who do not participate in other activities.

19) In addition to your regular reminiscent group, reminiscing is a great activity to use when your planned activity falls through.

20) Relax! Even if you've never held a group before, use these tips and enjoy learning about the era your residents remember so very well.

GOOD OLD DAYS

Songs, Entertainment, Press, Movies, Transportation

1910-1920

By Dr. H.E. Klepinger

Dr. Klepinger, who died a few years ago while in his 80's, practiced medicine in Lafayette, Indiana for many, many years. His mind remained sharp and active till the end. He devised the following lists for me that will prove useful in involving the elderly in lively discussions of days gone by.

WE SANG

Let Me Call You Sweetheart
By the Light of the Silvery Moon
Down By the Old Mill Stream
When You Wore a Tulip
There's a Long, Long Trail
St. Louis Blues

WE LAUGHED

Charlie Chaplin

WE READ

The *Titanic* sank by iceberg
Haley's comet
Lusitania sank by German sub

WE SAW

The Perils of Pauline

WE TRAVELED

Horse and buggy
Street car

Page 111

GOOD OLD DAYS

Songs, Entertainment, Press, Movies, Transportation

1920-1930

WE SANG

Swanee
Margie
Sleepy Time Gal
Star Dust
Look for the Silver Lining
I'm Forever Blowing Bubbles
Alice Blue Gown
Always
Dinah

WE LAUGHED

Mr. Gallagher, Mr. Shean
Will Rogers
The Marx Brothers

WE READ

Women win right to vote
Radio broadcasting starts
Prohibition becomes law
Charles Lindbergh flies to France

WE SAW

Charlie Chaplin and Jackie Coogan in *The Kid.*

WE TRAVELED

Model T

GOOD OLD DAYS

Songs, Entertainment, Press,
Movies, Transportation
1930-1940

WE SANG

Tip Toe Through the Tulips
Somewhere Over the Rainbow
Stormy Weather
Summertime
September Song

WE LAUGHED

Amos and Andy
Fred Allen
Fibber McGee and Molly

WE READ

Lindbergh baby kidnapped
The Great Depression
Prohibition repealed
John Dillinger
Social security become law

WE SAW

Mutiny on the Bounty
Snow White

WE TRAVELED

Model A

GOOD OLD DAYS

**Songs, Entertainment, Press,
Movies, Transportation**
1940-1950

WE SANG

Oh Johnny!
Sentimental Journey
Blues in the Night

WE LAUGHED

Knock, knock. Who's there?
Edgar Bergen and Charlie McCarthy

WE READ

Germany invades
Pearl Harbor bombed
Penicillin perfected
Nylon introduced
United Nations founded

WE TRAVELED

Chevy

HELPFUL HINTS
FROM THE 19TH CENTURY

Never trim a lamp with scissors. It is almost impossible to cut it clean and straight. Just rub the burned part off with an old cloth.

Three or four cloves added to a cup of tea will relieve a headache almost immediately.

A quickly made glue is obtained by rubbing a little piece of cold boiled potato on a sheet of paper with the fingers.

Eggs that are to be kept should be stood on the small end and not the broad end.

To obtain a really good cup of coffee, place the coffee in a saucer and put it in a fairly hot oven for about three minutes before making. This brings out the flavor.

To make glassware glisten, wash the glass in hot water and then plunge into cold water to which a handful of starch has been dissolved. Drain the glassware on towels until perfectly dry, after which polish with a dry cloth.

To soften boots, wash them with warm water and then rub them with castor oil thoroughly. This makes the boots soft and elastic. Any other sort of oil will work, but castor is the best.

Equal parts of ammonia and turpentine will take paint out of clothing no matter how hard or dry. Saturate the spot two or three times and afterwards wash out with soap suds.

To remove red ink stains from table linen, spread freshly-made mustard over the stain and leave for half an hour. Then sponge off and all trace of the ink will have disappeared.

If a lump of sugar is put in the teapot when making tea, one spoonful of tea can be dispensed with.

Match marks on a polished surface may be removed by being first rubbed with a cut lemon and then with a rag dipped in cold water.

Pour boiling water over raisins, let stand for a few minutes, drain the water off, and you will find that the stones can be quickly and easily squeezed out from the stem end.

To remove grease stains from a tiled hearth, mix a strong solution of washing soda with some fuller's earth. Apply the paste to the hearth and leave for about an hour. Afterward wash off with hot soapy water.

To clean and polish old furniture make a mixture of a quart of old beer or vinegar with a handful of common salt and a tablespoon of muriatic acid and boil it for fifteen minutes; put it in a bottle and warm it when wanted for use. Wash the furniture you wish to clean with soft hot water so as to remove all the dirt then afterward wash it with the mixture in the bottle; then polish with a soft rag.

To clean looking glasses, remove with a damp sponge, fly stains and other soils (the sponge may be damped with water or spirits of wine. After this, dust the surface with the finest sifted whiting or powder-blue, and polish with a silk handkerchief or soft cloth. Snuff of candle, if quite free from grease, is an excellent polish for looking glasses.

To destroy cockroaches, mix together thoroughly one pound of powdered sugar, one pound of powdered borax and ten cents worth of *Paris Green*. Put in all places where they are seen with a small bellows or puffer.

Hair wash: The best wash we know for cleansing and softening the hair is an egg beaten up and rubbed well into the hair and afterwards washed out with several rinses of water.

To curl the hair take borax, two ounces; gum arabic, one drachm; and hot water, not boiling, one quart; stir. And as soon as the ingredients are dissolved add three tablespoons of strong spirits of camphor. On retiring to rest, wet the hair with the above liquid and roll in twists of paper as usual. Do not disturb the hair until morning. When you untwist it, it will form in ringlets.

To mend holes in stockings or merino underwear, tack a piece of net over the rent and darn through it.

To remove sunburn and prevent the skin from cracking melt two ounces of spermaceti in a pipkin, add two ounces of oil of almonds. When they are well mixed and have begun to cool, stir in a tablespoonful of fine honey and continue to stir briskly until cool. Put in small jars. Apply it on going to bed, after washing the face, and allow it to remain on all night.

It is said that strawberries rubbed over the face at night will remove freckles and sunburn.

Cure for chapped lips: dissolve a lump of beeswax in a small quantity of sweet oil over a candle. Let it cool, and it will be ready for use. Rubbing it warm on the lips two or three times will effect a cure.

Baths for children should be given according to age and constitution. Some require warm baths and cannot stand the effects of cold water, while with other children, it agrees perfectly. A tepid bath is the one most generally suitable. Young children should have their bath in the morning, and if they are under two years, may take it after their first meal. A child should never be given a hot bath in a very cold room, and thorough drying after bathing is of great importance.

To clean floor cloth, shred half an ounce of good beeswax into a saucer, cover it entirely with turpentine and place it in the oven until melted. After washing the floor cloth thoroughly with flannel, rub the whole surface lightly with a flannel dipped in the wax and turpentine, then rub with a dry cloth. Beside the polish produced, the surface is lightly coated with the wax, which is washed off together with any dust or dirt it may have contracted while the floor cloth is preserved. Milk is also very useful for cleaning floor cloth, applied after the usual washing with a damp cloth and it should then be rubbed over with a dry one.

Hard soap. Use three pounds of grease, one pound of *Babbit's* potash, ten quarts of water, one-half pound of borax; boil four or five hours, pour into a square wooden box, and when cold cut into blocks and set away to dry.

To clean combs--if it can be avoided, never wash combs as the water often makes the teeth split, and the tortoise shell or horn of which they are made, rough. Small brushes manufactured purposely for cleaning combs may be purchased at a trifling cost; with this the comb should be well brushed, and afterward wiped with a clot or towel.

***

These hints have been taken from a 19th century newspaper and from an old cookbook (without cover or title intact) that belonged to an 88-year-old resident of a nursing home. She began her marriage in 1917 with this cookbook which had belonged to her mother. The following cake recipe is from the same cookbook.

RICH BRIDE'S CAKE OR CHRISTENING CAKE FROM 19TH CENTURY

5 pounds of the finest flour,
3 pounds of fresh butter
5 pounds of currants
2 pounds of sifted loaf sugar
2 nutmegs
1/4 ounce of mace
1/4 ounce of clove
16 eggs
1 pound of sweet almonds
1/2 pound of candied citron
1/2 pound each of candied orange and lemon peel
1 gill of wine
1 gill of brandy

Let the flour be as fine as possible and well dried and sifted; the currants washed, picked and dried before the fire; the sugar well pounded and sifted; the nutmegs grated; the spices pounded; the eggs thoroughly whisked, whites and yolks separately; the almonds pounded with a little orange-flower water; and the candied peel cut in neat slices.

When all these ingredients are prepared, mix them in the following manner: Begin working the butter with the hand till it becomes of a cream-like consistency; stir in the sugar, and when the whites of the eggs are whisked to a solid froth, mix them with the butter and sugar; next well beat up the yolks for ten minutes and adding them to the flour, nutmegs, mace and cloves, continue beating the whole together for half an hour or longer, till wanted for the oven.

Then mix lightly the currants, almonds and candied peel with the wine and brandy; and having lined a hoop with buttered paper, fill it with the mixture and bake the cake in a tolerably quick oven, taking care, however, not to burn it; to prevent this, the top of it may be covered with a sheet of paper. To ascertain whether the cake is done, plunge a clean knife into the middle of it, withdraw it directly, and if the blade is not sticky and looks bright, the cake is sufficiently baked.

These cakes are usually spread with a thick layer of almond icing and over that another layer of sugar icing and afterward, ornamented. In baking a large cake like this, great attention must be paid to the heat of the oven; it should not be too fierce, but have moderate heat to bake the cake through.

Page 121

SILLY CRAZES AND FADS
OVER THE YEARS

Flag pole sitting
Pantie raids
Kissing contests
Ten-cent chain letter
Miniature golf
Swing music and swing language
Dance-a-thons
Rocking chair derbies
Eating contests
Mah-jongg
Crossword puzzles
Bridge
Daniel Boone caps
Mohawk haircuts
Hula-hoops
Cross-country racing
Wing-walking
Goldfish swallowing
Sock hops
Shirley Temple craze
White bucks
Burma Shave signs
Roller skating derbies
Yo-yo's
Pegged jeans
Stuffing gum in mouth (40 sticks)
Phone booth stuffing (31 men)
Piling men on a bed (55 men)
Volkswagen stuffing
Zoot suits

PRICES IN THE GOOD OLD DAYS
1935 Restaurant Menu

Soup and bread -- 5 cents
Two eggs/potatoes/coffee -- 10 cents
Pigs feet and kraut -- 10 cents
Pork tenderloin/drink -- 15 cents
Corn beef and cabbage -- 20 cents
Roast sirloin of beef -- 20 cents
Vienna roast and peas -- 10 cents
Lamb stew -- 15 cents
Hamburger steak -- 15 cents
Meatballs and beans -- 10 cents

MISCELLANEOUS PRICES -- 1930's

Milk -- 5-10 cents a quart
Sugar -- 5 cents a pound
Butter -- 28 cents a pound
Coffee --35 cents a pound
Bacon 35 cents a pound
Eggs -- 7 cents dozen
Bananas -- 7 cents a pound
Razor blades --10 for 49 cents
Silk necktie -- 55 cents
Dental filling -- $1.00
2-wheel bike -- $10.95
9 x 12 wool rug -- $5.85
Silk Stockings -- 69 cents
3 piece bedroom suite -- $49.95
Interurban ride -- 1 cent per mile
8-piece dining room set -- $46.50
Double bed, springs and mattress -- $14.95
Around the world by ship, 85 days, 14 countries -- $749.00

Milk-- 10 gallons from farm --$1.00
Sugar --$5 for 100 pounds
Ham -- 31 cents a pound
Corn Flakes -- 8 ounces for 8 cents
Bread -- $1 for 6 loaves
Sirloin -- 29 cents a pound
Shirt --47 cents
Gas Stove -- $23.95
Pullover sweater -- $1.95
Electric iron $1.95
Gasoline -- 11 cents a gallon
Land -- $35 an acre
1935 Chevy coup -- $659
1930 Studebaker -- $840

WE REMEMBER THE TWENTIES

by Marge Knoth

The roaring 20's was a decade like none other. The First World War was over and people wanted some fun. Automobiles certainly helped. Thanks to Henry Ford's assembly line, they were now becoming affordable to the common man. In fact, in 1919 alone, Ford produced 7 million of them, and by 1929, 23 million. They were not without their drawbacks, though. Ministers preached against their use by young people calling them "brothels on wheels." America was indeed losing her innocence.

Though the life expectancy was just 58 years, many folks sought to fill those years with immense pleasure. Motorcycles with side cars sped about. People developed a passion for flying and loved the many newspaper and magazine articles about it. Records were being set daily. Lindbergh had the eyes of the world on him as he completed his historical flight across the Atlantic in 1927. Rear Admiral Byrd and Floyd Bennett made the first successful flight over the North Pole in 1926. The Zeppelin circumnavigated the earth in 21 days and 7 hours.

Radio fast became a household necessity. In 1922, its sales amounted to $60 million, and by 1929 a whopping $850 million. Many people bought kits and made their own. Victrolas and player pianos graced parlors. The generation entertained themselves with other things, too: pogo sticks, bridge, Mahjongg, the just-new crossword puzzle book, hot sea baths and magazines. *True Story,* alone, sold two-million copies. *Liberty,* a highly controversial magazine, came out in the '20's and lasted until 1950. They also enjoyed wild things like flag-pole sitting and wing walking.

Young people never tired of tea dances held on Saturday afternoons where they melted together in each other's arms, cheek against cheek, shuffling about the dance floor. The *black bottom* dance was popular, joining the *charleston* and the *tango.* Dance-a-thons for prize money sometimes lasted for days. Girls regularly shed their corsets in dance hall rest rooms because it was rumored boys didn't dance with girls who wore corsets. The clergy denounced the new dancing as "syncopating embracing."

Much to their father's dismay, young women sacrificed their beautiful long hair to crazy short bobs. Electric perms, where women were wired up to a monstrous machine, became the rage. Gals wore minus skirts which revealed rolled-down silk stockings beneath their rouged knees. They smoked cigarettes and slopped around with unbuckled galoshes. They also wore cloche hats and hobble skirts which made walking difficult. Long raccoon coats were worn by both men and women. In the '20's, bosoms were flattened until 1929 when Polly Peabody invented the bra. She simply tied two handkerchiefs together and sewed on a pink bow. Warner Brothers bought the patent for $15,000.

Stock market prices tripled between 1925 and 1929. Folks, even the common man, invested freely. The national income rose some 40% between 1922 and 1929--from $60.7 billion to $87.2 billion. The U.S. population increased by 17,492,280 between 1920 and 1930 bringing it from 105,710,620 to a grand 123,203,000. The decade saw four presidents: Wilson, Harding, Hoover and Coolidge. Henry Ford established the five-day work week for his employees.

The 18th amendment in 1920 introduced prohibition with the *National Prohibition Act* called the *Volstead Act*. Rather than curtailing the drinking of liquor, it led to the rise of the speakeasy, an illegal bar. Many made their own beer and liquor at home. In fact, bootlegging generated an estimated $3,600,000,000.

Margaret Sanger shocked the world when she wrote an article in her magazine the *Woman Rebel* about the need to limit the birth rate. When she opened a clinic in Brooklyn to share birth control information, she was promptly closed down and sent to jail for 30 days. The charge was obscenity.

Page 125

News of the day told of the deaths of Annie Oakley, and of Rudolf Valentino who was called the "the great lover." Actress Clara Bow was the "it" girl of the '20's. Mary Pickford was everybody's sweetheart. The Ziegfield Follies featured long lines of beautiful dancing girls among other acts. Gertrude Eberle, at age 19, was the first woman to swim the English Channel. Margaret Gorman won the first Miss America contest which was held in Washington D.C. in 1921. She had only seven competitors.

The Ku Klux Klan marched on Washington and were feared by many. Two-million rural Americans joined the Klan. King Tut's tomb was discovered in 1922. Florida saw a horrible hurricane that killed 372 people. A horrible tornado hit the midwestern states in 1924 wiping out 35 towns. Before it was finished, 800 were dead and 15,000 were homeless. The good times quickly came to an end on that fateful day of October 24, 1929 when the stock market crashed and $4 billion dollars in paper values were lost in a day.

The 20's, a decade our residents may well remember, was a time of searching and a time of discovery. A lifestyle unknown to other decades unfolded before their eyes. It was a happy time, a fun time, a prosperous time--and finally a sad time. But while it lasted, life was fast and full in the roaring '20's.

***

Library of Congress, National Archives

Page 127

IN ACCOUNT WITH

LAFAYETTE HOME HOSPITAL

LAFAYETTE, IND.. _April 14,_ 19 3_6_

TO _Master Herbert Heim_

726 No. Main St., W.L.

ROOM _236_

Terms—All Bills Must Be Secured in Advance. A Statement of Accounts Will Be Rendered Weekly.

Dr. Calvert DESCRIPTION	CHARGES	
Balance Acct. Rendered		
Room and Care _20 days @ $4.00_	$80	00
Medication _20 days @ 10¢_	2	00
Operating Room	2	00
Delivery Room		
Care of Infant		
X-Ray		
Dressing	4	00
Drugs	9	60
Laboratory Fee and Path. Exam.	6	00
Special Nurse Board		
Anesthetic		
Cast		
Guest Trays		
Cot		
Total	$103	60
Credits _Broken dishes_	1	55
Balance Amount Due ☞	$105	15
	50	00
	$55	15

Page 128

Other Books by the Author

Newsletters Simplified! Don't let the name mislead you. Its 352 pages are packed full of fascinating information for newsletters--YES! But it's ALSO for those who lead activities; for those who like to impress friends with unusual tidbits of information; for those who like history or nostalgia; and for those who enjoy reading and learning. Included are: five great chapters on writing; layout and design; article types; proofreading; marketing; and more. **BUT THAT'S JUST THE BEGINNING.** You'll find another 12 chapters of information to include "in" your newsletter. These consist of: startling facts; statistics and tidbits; presidential anecdotes and presidential trivia; quotable quotes; helpful hints; facts about historical celebrities (Lindbergh, Earhart, Rockwell, Will Rogers, Shirley Temple, Dionne Quintuplets, Teddy Roosevelt, John Dillinger). You'll also find complete reminiscent articles to print in your newsletter; a rich history of 55 holidays and holy days; funny stories and interesting experiences related by seniors; old-time prices; 15 pages of *Do You Remember?* one liners; comforting scriptures; and 15 full-page historical photographs.
ISBN 0-927935-06-6. **$19.99** plus shipping.

Activity Planning at Your Fingertips provides all the activities you'll ever need. Over 600 are presented with complete directions for each. Also featured are three years of pre-planned activity calendars that you are free to copy and use. *Activity Planning at Your Fingertips* is a user-friendly guide created especially for the busy professional who's short on time but desires to be long on activities. The book is divided into ten tabbed sections, and then each section is alphabetized to help you locate any activity in just seconds. There's activity ideas for bedside residents, for low-functioning residents and for more alert and active residents. There's holiday parties; family parties; cooking; crafts; exercise; games; word games; fill-ins; Christmas; men only; outings; clubs; community outreaches; special projects; monthly biggies; and everyday activities. It's a big 208 pages, professionally wiro-bound, ISBN 0-927935-03-01. **$28.99** plus shipping.

The Professional Activity Director is a complete handbook covering most subjects pertinent to activity directors. These include: recognizing and developing your professionalism; getting great press coverage; organizing your department; calendar planning made easy; involving your community in your activities; developing and maintaining a workable volunteer program; beating burnout; handling problems common to A.D.'s; planning interesting outings for residents; building an incubator and hatching chicks; planning a district-wide nursing home olympics; word games; a host of new activity ideas; special helps for A.D.'s; and much more. ISBN 0-927935-00-7. **$15.99** plus shipping.

Looking Back, Reminiscent Party Fun for Senior Citizens. Features 200 questions and answers about the good old days which are sure to excite your residents. It is great for entertaining residents while they are waiting for lunch to be served and for when your planned entertainment doesn't show up. Also for leading lively reminiscent groups, and for one-on-one activity with residents. Sample questions: *Why did the old kitchen stove have to be blackened regularly?* (To keep it from rusting.) *Why did early movies never show close-ups of people?* (They felt viewers would feel cheated seeing only half a person.) ISBN 0-927935-01-5 **$10.99** plus shipping.

Books may be ordered from Valley Press, P.O. Box 5224, Lafayette, IN 47903, Phone 317-447-5592, Fax, 317-449-0406